BIOMEDICAL ENGINEERING
AND Human Body Systems

Crabtree Publishing Company

www.crabtreebooks.com

Rebecca Sjonger

Crabtree Publishing Company

www.crabtreebooks.com

Author: Rebecca Sjonger

**Publishing plan research
and development:** Reagan Miller

Photo research: James Nixon

Editors: Paul Humphrey, James Nixon,
Kathy Middleton

Consultant: Carolyn De Cristofano, M.Ed.
STEM consultant, Professional Development Director
of Engineering is Elementary (2005-2008)

Proofreader: Wendy Scavuzzo

Layout: sprout.uk.com

Cover design and logo: Margaret Amy Salter

**Production coordinator and prepress
technician:** Margaret Amy Salter

Print coordinator: Margaret Amy Salter

Written and produced for Crabtree Publishing Company
by Discovery Books

Photographs:
Alamy: p. 4 (ZUMA Press, Inc).
Bigstock: pp. 8 (geniebird), 9 bottom (Reflektastudios),
11 bottom (E. Hoffmann), 13 top (CHEN WEI SENG),
14 (Wavebreak Media Ltd), 15 top (NikD51), 15 bottom
(leaf), 17 (a_mikos), 19 left (alexmit), 19 right (viczast),
23 top (Baloncici), 23 bottom (Kasia Bialasiewicz),
24 (clara), 25 bottom (Click and Photo), 27 (wrangle).
Dr. Max Ortiz Catalan, Chalmers University of Technology:
pp. 16, 18, 20.
Getty Images: pp. 9 top (Kenneth Garrett), 11 top (Michael
Friberg/Contour), 12 (Richard Saker/Contour), 21 (Steve
Russell/Toronto Star), 22 (Ute Grabowsky/Photothek),
25 top (Andrew Stawicki/Toronto Star), 28 (Jeff J.
Mitchell), 29 (JEAN-PHILIPPE KSIAZEK/AFP).
Jacobs School of Engineering/UC San Diego: p. 5.
Shutterstock: front cover: © bikeriderlondon (right);
© Alexander Raths (bottom right); © Olesia Bilkei
(top left); © Lightspring (background).
The University of Washington: p. 10 (Stephen Brashear).
Wikimedia: front cover middle left, pp. 7 (Connexions), 13
bottom (Petty Officer 2nd Class Greg Mitchell of the US
Navy), 26 (Chittka L. Brockmann).

Library and Archives Canada Cataloguing in Publication

Sjonger, Rebecca, author
Biomedical engineering and human body systems /
Rebecca Sjonger.

(Engineering in action)
Includes index.
Issued in print and electronic formats.
ISBN 978-0-7787-7505-8 (bound).--
ISBN 978-0-7787-7526-3 (paperback).--
ISBN 978-1-4271-9997-3 (pdf).--ISBN 978-1-4271-9993-5 (html)

1. Biomedical engineering--Juvenile literature. 2. Human
biology--Juvenile literature. I. Title. II. Series: Engineering in
action (St. Catharines, Ont.)

R856.2.S56 2015   j624.1'51   C2015-903389-6
                                            C2015-903390-X

Library of Congress Cataloging-in-Publication Data

Sjonger, Rebecca, author.
Biomedical engineering and human body systems /
Rebecca Sjonger.
pages cm. -- (Engineering in action)
Includes index.
ISBN 978-0-7787-7505-8 (reinforced library binding) --
ISBN 978-0-7787-7526-3 (pbk.) --
ISBN 978-1-4271-9997-3 (electronic pdf) --
ISBN 978-1-4271-9993-5 (electronic html)
1. Medical technology--Juvenile literature. 2. Medical innovations--
Juvenile literature. I. Title. II. Series: Engineering in action.

R855.4.S56 2016
610.28--dc23
                                        2015017923

Crabtree Publishing Company
www.crabtreebooks.com   1-800-387-7650

Printed in Canada/082015/BF20150630

Published in Canada
Crabtree Publishing
616 Welland Ave.
St. Catharines, ON
L2M 5V6

Published in the United States
Crabtree Publishing
PMB 59051
350 Fifth Avenue, 59th Floor
New York, New York 10118

Published in the United Kingdom
Crabtree Publishing
Maritime House
Basin Road North, Hove
BN41 1WR

Published in Australia
Crabtree Publishing
3 Charles Street
Coburg North
VIC, 3058

CONTENTS

WHAT IS BIOMEDICAL ENGINEERING?

Doctors and other healthcare experts improve and save people's lives every day. Biomedical engineers make their work possible. Like other kinds of engineers, they use math, science, and creative ideas to solve challenges. These engineers also understand human body systems. Their work helps doctors detect, treat, and prevent medical problems. For example, one kind of biomedical engineer may design an x-ray machine that shows broken bones inside bodies. The bones may then be repaired with special metal pins and rods developed by a different kind of biomedical engineer.

EIGHT STEPS TO SUCCESS

Biomedical engineers follow a design process, or series of steps. It makes sure new tools, treatments, or systems are the best and safest they can be for the people who will use them. Engineers follow these steps to design, build, and test models.

The heart-lung machine is a biomedical engineering innovation. When a patient's heart and lungs are stopped during surgery, this machine does their work outside of the patient's body.

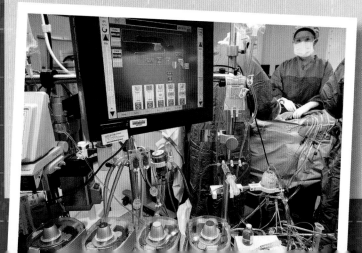

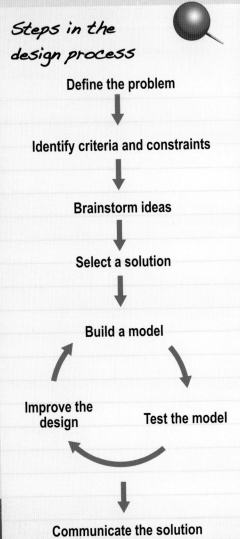

Steps in the design process

Define the problem

↓

Identify criteria and constraints

↓

Brainstorm ideas

↓

Select a solution

↓

Build a model

↓

Test the model

Improve the design

↓

Communicate the solution

Scientists and engineers: There is a close link between biomedical science and engineering. They are not the same, however. Scientists study the human body and medical problems, such as **infectious diseases**. They investigate how a disease moves from person to person. Their research helps engineers take action. Engineers design, test, and build practical ways to solve problems. They can develop a new tool or system to prevent a disease from spreading.

American Yuan-Cheng Fung received the National Medal of Science in 2000. It honored his work in science and engineering.

YUAN-CHENG FUNG

Yuan-Cheng Fung was born in China. In his twenties, he moved to the United States to attend the California Institute of Technology. He taught aircraft engineering there in the 1950s. Around that time, his mother developed a medical condition that causes vision loss. To help her get better treatment, Fung investigated her condition. That led him to study other medical problems and the human body. Fung left aircraft engineering and started a new field called **biomechanics**—a science that views the body as a machine. This area became one part of bioengineering. Bioengineering combines engineering practices with the study of living things. Biomedical engineering is also part of bioengineering. It focuses on developing technologies to solve people's health problems.

THE HUMAN BODY

The human body is a system. A system is a set of related parts that work together. Inside the body, there are smaller systems, which are sometimes called subsystems. The **tissues** and **organs** that make up the systems are body materials and parts formed by groups of cells. A cell is the smallest functioning unit in a living thing. You would need a microscope to see one. Each part of the body has a function, or job to do. The systems they belong to must interact for the body to work properly. For example, your **nervous system** and your **respiratory system** work together to allow you to breathe. Biomedical engineers design solutions that help the human body perform at its best.

See your systems work together: Do you want to see your nervous, muscular, and **skeletal systems** in action? First, find a ruler and a friend to help you. One person will grasp the top of the ruler with his or her thumb and pointer finger, and hold it up in the air. The other person will place his or her hand about a fist-length below the bottom of the ruler. Their fingers and thumb should be ready to grip the ruler. The person holding the ruler lets go of it without warning. The catcher grabs it as quickly as he or she can. Note the level the hand is touching. Repeat all the steps. Was your reaction time faster or slower the second time? Change places and compare your speeds.

When your friend drops the ruler, your eyes send a signal, or message, to your brain. Your brain decides what to do and sends a message to your hand. Your muscles and bones work together to catch the ruler. They should react faster with practice.

Circulatory system

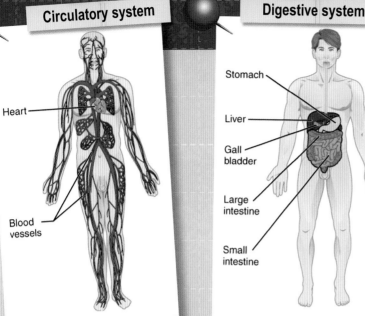

Heart

Blood vessels

The function of the circulatory system is to carry blood throughout the body. The heart and blood vessels belong to this system.

Digestive system

Stomach

Liver

Gall bladder

Large intestine

Small intestine

The digestive system takes in food and breaks it down for use in the body.

Nervous system

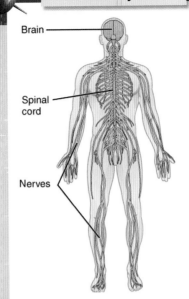

Brain

Spinal cord

Nerves

The nervous system sends messages throughout the body. This information travels to and from the brain.

Respiratory system

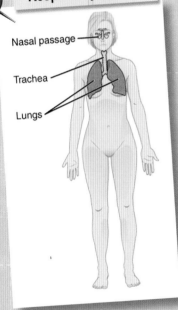

Nasal passage

Trachea

Lungs

The respiratory system brings oxygen into the body and removes carbon dioxide. The lungs are an important pair of organs in this system.

Muscular system

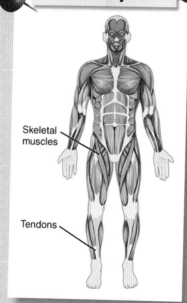

Skeletal muscles

Tendons

One function of the muscular system is to move the body. Tissues called tendons connect bones to the skeletal muscles.

Skeletal system

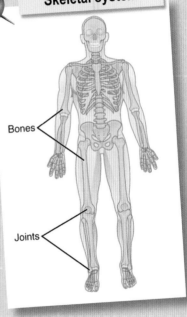

Bones

Joints

Bones in the skeletal system shape and support the body. This system includes ligaments, which are tissues that connect bones together.

HISTORICAL DEVICES AND DISCOVERIES

Pioneers throughout history have found ways to solve medical problems. Modern inventions are often new versions of old discoveries. For example, ancient Egyptians used hollow reeds to hear inside a body. Thousands of years later, a doctor in France rolled up his newspaper to listen to the sounds inside a patient's chest. These basic ideas led to the stethoscope. In ancient China, wheelbarrows carried people as well as objects. Eventually, this idea developed into a wheelchair.

CENTURIES OF PROGRESS

People in ancient times knew that looking through curved glass made it easier to see close up or far away. One thousand years ago in Egypt, Ibn al-Haytham wrote about how light enters the eyes. His theories described how eyes function in the nervous system. Soon after, eyeglasses were invented. Who first made them and when is unknown. They were used in China in the 1200s and in Europe soon after. In 1604, a German astronomer named Johannes Kepler explained exactly how glasses allow eyes to see more clearly. As scientists learned more about eye health, engineers designed useful technological solutions to eye problems. Now we have equipment to check a person's vision. Contact lenses may be worn instead of glasses. Laser surgery can even reshape parts of the eye and improve sight.

In 1851, German professor Hermann von Helmholtz designed a tool called an ophthalmoscope. It helps doctors assess the health of an eye.

Ancient innovations included artificial body parts. A toe made from leather and wood was found attached to a 3,000-year-old Egyptian mummy. The toe probably helped her balance as she walked.

INCUBATORS FOR NEWBORN BABIES

Just 100 years ago, babies who were born before they were due were unlikely to survive. One big challenge was keeping them warm after birth. In the 1880s, a French doctor solved this problem. While visiting the zoo, Dr. Stéphane Tarnier saw a device that kept newly hatched chicks warm. He was inspired to build something similar for babies. His first **incubator** held multiple babies, just like a group of chicks. Designs continued to improve over the years. For example, large metal incubators were switched to glass, so parents could see inside. Modern biomedical engineers have developed incubators that are easy to move. That means they can be used outside of hospitals.

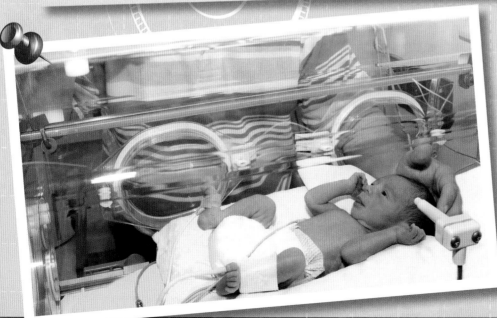

Modern incubators have armholes that allow people to reach in and handle babies lying inside the machines.

MODERN BIOMEDICAL ENGINEERS

All biomedical engineers use their knowledge of human health on the job. They also use a combination of computer, chemical, electrical, or mechanical engineering skills. No matter what their backgrounds are, solving problems in creative ways is the key to their roles. They need to be strong leaders who can work well in teams. Communication skills are also important because they interact with patients, medical experts, scientists, and other engineers. Here are just a few of the areas in which biomedical engineers work:

Hospitals: Engineers ensure that hospitals have the equipment needed to treat or monitor patients. This may mean designing new electronic devices. Engineers also work with existing equipment. They work with skilled technicians to ensure machines run smoothly. For example, **dialysis** machines do the work of **kidneys** when a person's kidneys stop functioning. Engineers consult with doctors who specialize in kidney health and their patients to improve dialysis machines.

Industry: Some engineers develop and test new products, such as gear for high-performance athletes. They often use biomechanics in their jobs. For example, they study **stress** on the muscular and skeletal systems of athletes in motion. They share the data with running-shoe designers. When final designs are ready, they can explain the engineering benefits to the team who will sell the products.

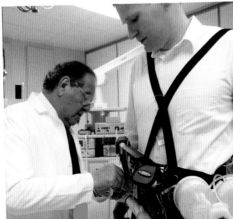

The invention of this wearable replacement kidney meant dialysis patients no longer had to spend so much time at the hospital.

Research: Researchers work in many places, including universities and drug companies. Engineers manage research projects that study medical problems and solutions. They also run labs and support other researchers. One growing area of research is **bionanotechnology**. It involves the study of the structures and functions of human body systems. The natural, machine-like designs of body parts give engineers ideas for nanotechnology (machines that are smaller than human cells). Nanotechnologies are an exciting new way to detect and treat diseases such as cancer.

The Nike Sports Research Lab studies the movements of elite athletes. This research results in advanced gear that helps people perform even better.

Biomedical engineering is the fastest-growing kind of engineering. There are opportunities in many areas, such as designing cochlear implants like this one.

Governments: Engineers who work for governments may be part of the team that **regulates**, or controls, biomedical products. These controls help protect the people who use the products. Checking that a proper design process is used is one way to keep devices and materials safe. Engineers also test new designs. For example, they regulate products like **cochlear implants**. These devices connect to the nervous system and help people with hearing loss. Before people were allowed to use them, government engineers had to evaluate whether they worked well and if they were safe.

STARTING THE DESIGN PROCESS

Successful design projects follow a well laid-out process. Some engineers manage or assist with each stage of the process. Other engineers focus on the areas in which they are experts. They may team up with other kinds of engineers, as well as doctors, scientists, and businesspeople. The process begins by clearly identifying the challenge. Engineers ask themselves, "What is the specific problem that needs solving?" or "What is the task that needs to be completed?"

Defining the problem: Some biomedical engineers design **prostheses.** These are replacement body parts. An upper limb prosthesis can include parts from the shoulders down the arms to the hands and fingers. One common kind is controlled by **electrodes.** These small devices direct electricity into and out of an object. They attach to the skin on the remaining part of the limb. The electrodes pick up signals when muscles beneath the skin move. The signals direct the actions of a prosthesis. These electrodes do not always understand the signals properly, however. In Sweden, a team led by biomedical engineer Max Ortiz Catalan set out to solve the problem of unreliable upper limb prostheses.

There are many kinds of prosthetic limbs. This replacement leg was built just for cycling.

Criteria and constraints

When the problem is defined, the next step is to figure out the details of the task. Before biomedical engineers consider any solutions, they gather facts. They identify the criteria, or needs, of a design. They also consider the constraints, or limits, of the project.

Some people are born missing body parts. Others lose them from illnesses or injuries.

If prosthetic arms do not work well or are uncomfortable, people may not wear them.

Investigating the problem: Max Ortiz Catalan's team in Sweden wanted the new prosthetic arm to function just like a healthy limb. Signals from the brain to the prosthesis needed to be clear and constant. It also had to be comfortable to wear all day. In addition to these criteria, there were some constraints:

· The link between the prosthesis and the nervous, muscular, and skeletal systems had to be safe for the user.

· The materials used had to work in normal conditions, such as cold, heat, sweat, and dirt.

· Prostheses are very expensive to design, so they would have to be a reasonable cost in the future.

BRAINSTORMING

After biomedical engineers have defined and researched a problem, they begin to explore many possible solutions. They come up with as many ideas as they can. No suggestion is too unrealistic at this stage. After recording all the ideas, more work goes into describing the ideas that seem most likely to work.

Exploring ideas: Looking at how a healthy arm works is a great way to start brainstorming ways to improve a prosthetic arm. The brain sends messages to the muscular system through the nerves. Then muscles, tendons, bones, and ligaments interact to move the arm. When electrodes are attached to a remaining part of a limb, they sense those movements under the skin. Based on mathematical calculations, the electrodes determine how to move the prosthesis. If the skin is too cold, dry, warm, or damp, signals may be distorted, or unclear. Where would you place the electrodes to get stronger signals from the brain? The team in Sweden thought joining the prosthesis directly to the nerves was a promising idea.

Brainstorming often works best when experts from different fields come up with ideas together. They think about things from many points of view.

INGENIUS IDEAS

Biomedical engineering has a history of turning ideas that sound outlandish into solutions that save lives.

Over 100 years ago, pioneers in heart health knew that the organ had its own electrical system. They had many ideas for how to send streams of electricity into the heart when the natural system failed. One experiment was powered by a car battery! In the 1960s, some of those ideas finally led to a solution. Artificial **cardiac pacemakers** were placed inside the body to set the rhythm of the faulty heart. Since then, there have been many advances in technology and the understanding of the heart. Engineers and doctors have worked together to improve the devices.

Another ingenious invention is **magnetic resonance imaging (MRI)**. Before the 1970s, doctors could not see some parts inside the human body. An idea to solve that problem came to American professor Paul Lauterbur while he was eating at a diner. He wrote his idea on a paper napkin! Using scientific research, he came up with a solution. It used a strong magnet and radio waves. Over time, a scanner was developed. A patient lies on a table, which slides inside a tunnel-like magnet. Radio waves help pick up magnetic signals from the body, which are sent to a computer. Images are created that show fine details inside the body.

This x-ray shows the placement of a pacemaker inside a body. These devices help hearts function properly.

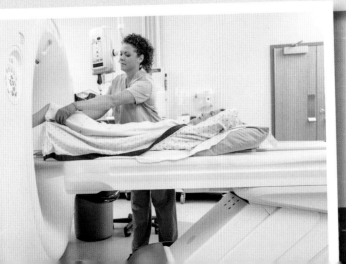

Doctors study MRI scans to detect many medical problems, such as damage to nerves, blood vessels, organs, and bones.

SELECTING A SOLUTION

In the next step of the process, the design team studies the most promising ideas from the brainstorming stage. They ask themselves which idea is most likely to work. They review the project criteria and constraints. After looking at all the pros and cons, they agree on a design or an approach to develop further.

Max Ortiz Catalan poses with a model hand that shows how the electrodes in his design work.

Choosing a design: The team in Sweden thought connecting a prosthesis directly to the nerves and muscles in the remaining limb was the solution that was most likely to work. The controls would get signals from the brain more reliably. With this approach, the prosthesis might even be designed to send messages back to the brain. Lightweight building materials, batteries, electronics, and motors were available. This would help to make the prosthetic arm more comfortable and usable for the user.

ATTACHING THE PROSTHESIS

How would you attach a prosthetic arm to the human body? The **socket** in an artificial limb usually connects it to the remaining part of a limb. The device is usually held in place with straps and a harness or through **suction**. With suction, the socket squeezes tightly over part of the remaining limb. This kind of socket has some problems. It can rub the skin, trap sweat, and even cause pain. Sockets can also cover up a joint, which is a point where two parts of the skeletal system fit together. The joint may then lose part of its ability to move. What if the new prosthetic arm used a more direct attachment system? A surgeon could implant, or insert, the connector into the body. This would completely eliminate the need for a socket.

Trade-offs

Possible **trade-offs** are also considered when selecting a design. A trade-off occurs when one feature is set aside so that a key criterion or constraint is met. For example, plans to attach the prosthetic arm directly to the remaining part of a limb came with a trade-off. With one bone bearing the load of the prosthesis, it could not also hold a large amount of extra weight. However, it was important to have the direct connection. The design gave up greater strength to make sure there was greater reliability.

This prosthetic leg is connected to the remaining part of the limb with a socket and straps.

BUILDING MODELS

Biomedical engineers build models called **prototypes** to help them predict how well designs will perform. Drawings detail what a prototype will look like. Prototype designs are also modeled using computers. Then full-size or **scale models** are made. They may be of the whole design or of just one part, if it is complex. Engineers do not expect the first few prototypes they build to be perfect. They will look for flaws during the testing stage.

Constructing a model: Designers of prostheses must test full-size, working prototypes. Creating them may require the help of electrical, computer, or mechanical engineers. In the case of Ortiz Catalan's prosthetic arm, a complete working prototype was made for a human test subject. To prepare, the subject had seven electrodes joined to muscles and nerves inside his body. The electrodes would send signals to and from the prosthetic arm.

Max Ortiz Catalan (left) and Rickard Brånemark (right) examine the model prosthetic arm attached to the test subject.

Design, test, refine

Part of the design process is a **cycle**, or a series of steps that repeat in the same order. To get the best possible results, engineers build, test, redesign, rebuild, and retest models. The steps repeat and trade-offs are made. Engineers continue with **optimization**, which means they make improvements until the design functions as well as possible. If the cycle keeps producing poor results, engineers return to the design selection step. The design process can take a lot of time and money. That is why most engineers focus on one solution at a time.

BONE AND METAL

Swedish researcher Per-Ingvar Brånemark experimented on rabbits in the 1950s. He placed titanium, a strong but lightweight metal, into their bones when he was studying blood flow. He discovered that as the rabbits' bones healed, they grew around the metal. Brånemark went on to use this process to create **dental implants**, which are artificial roots for human teeth. His son Rickard carried on his work in a new way. He uses his father's process to attach prostheses. In fact, Rickard Brånemark was the surgeon on the team designing the new prosthetic arm. He inserted a titanium rod into the test subject's remaining bone. Then bone cells grew around the rod. The surgeon also attached a metal clamp for connecting the prosthesis.

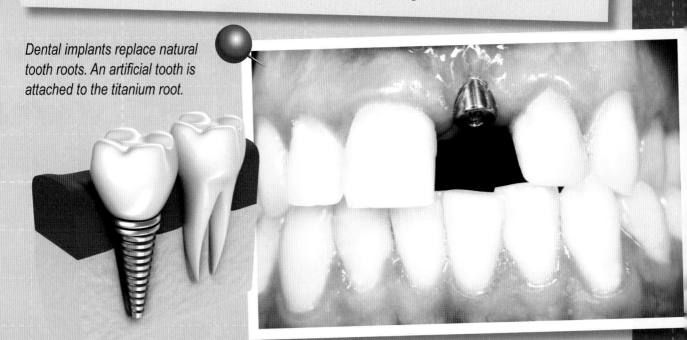

Dental implants replace natural tooth roots. An artificial tooth is attached to the titanium root.

TESTING MODELS

After a prototype is built, it is ready to be tried out in a variety of conditions. Field tests are run in the environments where the design will be used. Engineers collect data on how well the model performs during testing. They investigate all the possible problems to improve overall function. They must evaluate how well their prototypes meet the requirements of the project.

Test and assess: It was important to Ortiz Catalan that the new prosthetic arm was tested outside of the lab. He knew that people use prostheses differently at home than at work. He wanted to see how his design worked in a real-world setting. Evidence showed that the test subject's coordination improved. Moving the artificial arm took much less effort than moving his traditional electric arm. The prototype worked well in cold and hot conditions. The tester reported that he was able to return to working full time. He had even worn the replacement arm when sleeping, which is very unusual for someone with a prosthetic limb. One flaw was that for the prosthesis to send signals to the brain, it needed equipment only available in the lab. In addition, the trade-off for reliability was less strength than a natural arm. The team in Sweden wanted to see what would happen in the long term. Testing continued for almost two years before the first results were shared.

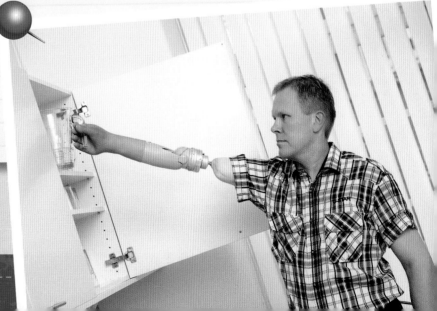

The test subject for the prosthetic arm design is known as Magnus N. He is a truck driver in Sweden.

MANY TESTS

Engineers test prototypes to find and fix faults in their designs. A model may also undergo other types of testing. In tests that involve patients, doctors help evaluate designs and collect results. Medical schools and hospitals may help run tests with human subjects. Businesses that will sell the tested products get involved to ensure the product is worth selling. They may consult with biomedical engineers. Governments do safety tests on final designs. Biomedical engineers may assist with government testing. Their goal is to protect people who buy or use products.

This team is designing a mouth guard for kids. Part of their prototype process includes **computer simulations**. These are tests run on computer models. They can show how a physical model might react under many different conditions.

IMPROVING DESIGNS

After engineers identify problems with the prototype, they develop ideas for redesign. A second run through the cycle begins. The goal is to make the design perform well with as few trade-offs as possible. They may discover that the idea they chose to develop does not solve the problem. Another solution is then selected and a new cycle begins.

Refine the design: The testing phase for the prosthetic arm developed in Sweden revealed ways in which it could be improved. Its ability to sense touch and send signals to the brain when the person was outside the lab needed more work. One solution was to add **sensors** to the hand. The device would react to pressure and temperature. Sensors can tell how much strength a hand is using. Another step toward refining the arm was to test it on other human subjects. More data needed to be collected. How would other test subjects respond to the attachment? There were still risks of infection and that the remaining bone might break under pressure.

Sensors on prosthetic hands help them be more life-like. They send signals to the brain that make it possible for an artificial hand to "feel" objects.

DANGEROUS DESIGNS

People could be injured or even die if design faults make it through the prototype stage. Serious problems have been found with some **automated external defibrillators**, or AEDs. These emergency medical devices help people whose hearts have stopped functioning properly. First, they check the rhythm of the heart. Then they reset a healthy rhythm by sending an electric shock to it. The U.S. Food and Drug Administration noticed an increased number of device failures. They ordered recalls, which are returns of products, for 70 kinds of AEDs from 2005 to 2009. Engineers and doctors studied the machines. They discovered faults in the designs. More thorough testing during the engineering design process might have found these problems before people were harmed.

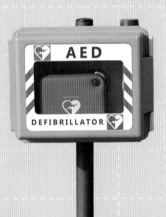

Today's improved AEDs are well designed. They are stored in public places. Anyone can use them in an emergency. They save more than 500 lives each year in the United States and Canada.

SUPPORT SYSTEM

During surgeries, **anesthetists** monitor the most important human body functions, such as heart rate and breathing. If anything goes wrong, they must react right away. A team of people from different fields in the Netherlands worked together on a patient assessment tool. They designed a system to help anesthetists make quick decisions during patient emergencies. In testing, the first prototype analyzed patient data to correctly identify the problem more than 90 percent of the time. For more detailed and accurate results, the system needed better mathematical formulas. A later prototype listed the top five problems a patient might have, in order of likelihood. The refined design was much more helpful as a decision-making support system.

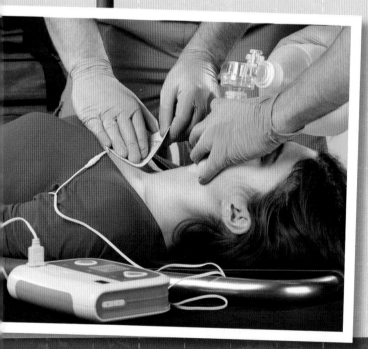

COMMUNICATING THE SOLUTION

Good communication skills are needed throughout the process. They are especially important when biomedical engineers need to present their results to other biomedical professionals. People who will benefit from the solution will also be interested. Incomplete solutions can also be shared because others can learn from them, too. Reviews of design problems and solutions appear in engineering, scientific, and medical journals, or magazines. Engineers also share the details of their design process at conferences, where people with common interests meet.

Telling the story: The next step for Ortiz Catalan's prosthetic arm was to continue work on the prototype and testing cycle. The final design would need to get government approval. But the results were already so exciting that they were shared in a science journal. The story spread around the world. The design and process was presented by his team in television, radio, online, and newspaper interviews. The attention could help create demand for the future product.

Conferences for biomedical engineers are held around the world each year. People gather to share new designs that help solve problems with the human body.

PROTOTYPE TO PRODUCTION

Many engineers want to share their solutions and improve people's lives around the world. First, their designs must meet government standards. After receiving government approval, engineers need to explain their designs clearly to the people who will make them. Some engineers also provide their technical knowledge to the businesses that will sell final products.

A camera pill is about the same size as a jellybean.

OTHER AMAZING SOLUTIONS

Biomedical engineers have designed many other solutions that improve people's lives. For example, camera pills travel through the digestive system taking photos. After a patient swallows a camera pill, a doctor checks the health of organs like the stomach. Another example is the **insulin pump** that works with a **glucose monitor**. This helps people with a disease called **diabetes**. Every day, people with diabetes must test the levels of a sugar called glucose in their blood. They may also need to inject insulin. Their health is at risk if their blood sugar levels drop or rise too much. The monitors and pumps do all the work for users, making life much easier and safer.

An insulin pump has electronic controls and a battery. In some designs, a tube delivers insulin from the pump. Other types of pumps are placed inside the body or stuck onto the skin.

25

DESIGN CHALLENGE

An ear is a complex structure. The outer part collects waves of sound. The inner parts vibrate and send signals to the nervous system. The brain receives the messages and figures out what the sound is. Biomedical engineers have helped create many devices to solve hearing problems.

It is time to try out your engineering skills! Using the eight steps of the design process, can you build a simple tool to help your outer ear pick up more sounds? You may only use these materials for the challenge:

- 1 or more sheets of paper, sized at least 8 ½ x 11 inches (216 x 279 mm)

- any kind of tape

- scissors

1: Define the problem: Start with the problem or task. You must design, build, and test a tool that will collect more sound waves and improve hearing.

2: Investigate criteria and constraints: Consider your criteria. What does your design need to do? Decide how you will know if your design works. You may want to measure your success by your ability to hear a distant sound or someone whispering. List your constraints or limits. For example, you have very few materials to use. To prevent injury, the tool must not enter the ear canal.

3: Brainstorm: Dream up as many ideas as you can. Look at the natural shape of ears—human and animal—to get you started. Then review your list and identify the most promising ideas.

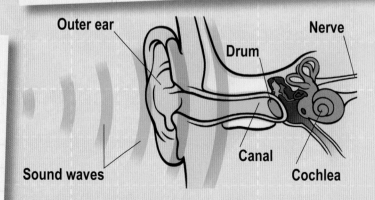

The parts of the inner ear help transmit sound waves to the brain.

4: Select a design: Evaluate your possible solutions. Remember to review your criteria and constraints. You should rule out ideas that use materials you do not have. Reject any ideas that could harm your ear. Choose the design you think is most likely to work well. Why do you think it will work?

5: Build a model: Sketch a diagram before making your prototype. You will probably want to make a full-size model. Do your best to build it, but remember that there are often flaws in the first model.

6: Test the model: In the second step, you decided how you would know if your design works. It's time to test it! Note which sounds you can hear with and without it. Repeat the tests to check your results. Invite friends to be test subjects.

Different animals have differently shaped ears that might inspire your design.

7: Improve the design: Were there any problems with your design? Even if it did work, can you improve it? It may need to be larger or differently shaped. If the first solution does not work, choose another idea to build and test.

8: Communicate the solution: Write a report, record a video, or prepare a live presentation that outlines each step of the process. Include diagrams and clear instructions. If you tried the challenge with a friend, present your findings to each other.

27

THE FUTURE OF THE FIELD

Some biomedical solutions commonly used today, such as MRIs, were unheard of just 50 years ago. The future will bring new designs that seem hard to believe now. People in wheelchairs may walk again because of the work being done with the nervous system. New medical tools will detect diseases earlier and provide better treatments. Sensors in our homes, cars, and phones could check our health throughout the day and alert us to possible problems.

Dr. Computer: Medical technologies are a very fast-growing area. Biomedical engineers are part of teams building computers that do some of the same work that doctors do. These computers will be able to sense a patient's symptoms, access all the related medical research, and decide on the best possible treatment. In the future, they may help doctors and improve the quality of patient care.

Biomedical engineers are trying to add the sense of touch to artificial body parts, so the brain can receive sensory signals from a prosthesis.

POWERFUL PRINTERS

Three-dimensional, or 3-D, printers create solid objects that have height, width, and depth. Since their first use in the 1980s, 3-D printers have become widely available. They print with many different materials, including plastics, powders, and metals. Engineers use them to print 3-D models and medical devices. They are testing many other ideas, too. Recently, a team printed replacement skull bone using special cement. **Bioprinting** is becoming an exciting part of the design process. Bioprinters use living cells from human bodies to create different tissues. Engineering students at the University of Toronto in Canada designed a prototype bioprinter that creates artificial skin. It may someday help doctors treat severe burns.

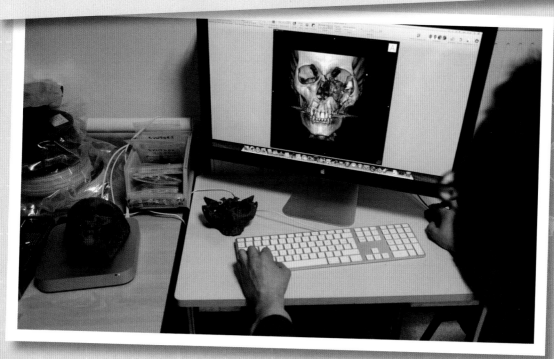

Body boosts

Designs created by biomedical engineers may also be applied to healthy human body systems. Would you like to see things that are only visible with microscopes or telescopes? Do you think it would be cool to pick up radio signals using only your ears? Would you like to try legs that were stronger than any human legs? These may all be possible in the future, thanks to engineers from different fields sharing their ideas. However, people argue over whether it is right or wrong to change the natural design of the human body. What do you think?

A 3-D printer can produce a replica of a human skull.

LEARNING MORE

BOOKS

Gray, Susan H. *Artificial Limbs*. Cherry Lake Publishing, 2008.

Jango-Cohen, Judith. *Bionics*. Lerner Publishing, 2006.

Mooney, Carla. *Medical Technology and Engineering*. Rourke Educational Media, 2012.

Richards, Jon. *The Human Body*. Owlkids, 2013.

Royston, Angela. *Heroes of Medicine and their Discoveries*. Crabtree Publishing, 2010.

Stewart, Melissa and Peter Bull. *How Is My Brain Like a Supercomputer? And Other Questions about the Human Body*. Sterling Children's Books, 2014.

ONLINE

www.sciencebuddies.org
Enter "biomedical engineer" in the search tool to access a career profile, project ideas, and news articles.

http://kidshealth.org/teen/your_body
Features a "Body Basics Library" that explains human body systems and important organs.

http://engineergirl.com
Explore this site for great information about engineering, or use the search tool to find out more about biomedical engineers.

www.youtube.com/watch?v=UKcSI_bZXB0
This minute-long animation shows how the design of the prosthetic arm highlighted in this book works.

PLACES TO VISIT

Biomedical Engineering Kiosk, Tampa, Florida
Play the role of a biomedical engineer when you visit this interactive educational kiosk. Collect and analyze data, diagnose the problem with a knee, then try out virtual surgical solutions.

www.digitalworlds.ufl.edu/projects/mosi/

GLOSSARY

anesthetist A medical professional who helps patients during surgeries by making sure they do not feel pain and monitoring their key body functions

automated external defibrillator (AED) A portable device that applies electricity to a heart that has stopped beating

biomechanics The study of forces on the human body

bionanotechnology The study of biology applied to the design of microscopic machines

bioprinting 3-D printing with living cells to create different tissues

cardiac pacemaker A medical device inserted into the body that sets the rhythm of the heart

cochlear implant A device connected to the nervous system that helps people hear

computer simulation A computer model that acts in a similar way to an actual object

cycle A series of steps that repeat in the same order

dental implant Artificial tooth roots created out of titanium

diabetes A disease that makes the body unable to produce enough insulin to control sugar levels in the blood

dialysis A medical process that does the work of kidneys if a person's kidneys stop functioning

electrode A small device that directs electricity into and out of an object

glucose monitor A device that measures the amount of sugar in a person's blood

incubator A warming device

infectious disease Serious illness that is spread from person to person

insulin pump A portable device that delivers insulin into a person's body

kidneys A pair of organs that form and release urine

magnetic resonance imaging (MRI) A system that uses magnet and radio waves to show details inside the body

nervous system The network of body parts, including the brain and nerves, that send and receive sensory information

optimization Improving a design to make it function as well as possible

organ A body part, such as the heart or lungs

pioneer The first person who develops an idea or technique

prostheses Artificial replacement body parts

prototype A model of a design built for testing

regulate To control or direct according to law

respiratory system The organs that work together to bring fresh air into a body and remove stale air

scale model A physical model that has the same proportions as the actual object but may be a different size

sensor A device that measures and responds to properties such as pressure or temperature

skeletal system The network of bones and connective tissues that shape and support a body

socket The hollow end of a prosthetic limb that connects it with the remaining part of a limb

stress Tension or pressure that is applied to an object

suction The act of sucking out air to create a tight seal

tissues Similar cells that form non-organ parts in the human body

trade-off The setting aside of one criterion so that another more important criterion is met

INDEX